To Emma
From
Brae
Lynne

DEDICATED TO MY FAMILY AND MY FUR FAMILY

ACKNOWLEDGEMENTS

I would like to thank my family and friends for always being there for me. Without them I don't know what I'd do.

FORWARD

I am nine years old and I wrote this book because I love dogs a lot. I have a dog and I love him very much. His name is Kaiser. He is a Bernese Mountain Dog and Bernese Mountain Dogs are big. Even though he is big, he thinks he's a lap dog.

The Beagle is a small dog that is black, brown and white. Male Beagles weigh 22-25 pounds and Females weigh 20-23 pounds. Beagles can be 13-16 inches tall. A Beagles life span is 12-15 years. They have a short coat and have a hard coat that's medium. They are originally from Great Britain.

Bernese Mountain Dog

I have a Bernese Mountain Dog and his name is Kaiser. These big dogs are originally from Switzerland and are working dogs. I would describe Kaiser as being playful, energetic, bouncy and goofy. When my Dad comes home from work, Kaiser will get excited and will start jumping around. Bernese Mountain Dogs (a.k.a. Bernese) are mostly black. They have rusty brown on the feet, cheeks, above the eyes and below the tail. There's also white on the tip of the tail, tips of the paws on the neck, chest and starting from the forehead down to the nose.

Boston Terrier

Boston Terriers are small black and white dogs. They're life span is 11-15 years of age. The litter size is 4-6 puppies. They originated from the United States. Boston Terriers are 10-25 pounds and are about 15-17 inches. Boston Terriers have a muzzle that's short and have no wrinkles. I know two Boston Terriers named Hogan and Temple. Temple is really calm and Hogan is energetic.

Boxer

Boxers are tall dogs with a short muzzle and a short tail. Males weigh 66-70 pounds and females weigh 55-60 pounds. Their coat is short, smooth and shiny. Their colour can be fawn or brindle. They can also have a black mask and white markings. Life span is 9-10 years. The average litter size is 6-8 puppies.

Brussels Griffon

The Brussels Griffon are intelligent, alert, sensitive and proud. Brussels Griffon are a member of the toy group. The facial features that characterize Brussels Griffon are largely the result of the spaniel strain. A Brussels Griffon played a leading role in the movie, As Good As It Gets, and the breed acquired fame. The Brussels Griffon's distinctive face is upturned, large and round. It can either have a rough coat or a smooth coat. They can come in the colours rich red, beige, black and tan, and all black, with occasional white spots or blaze on any coloured coat.

Bulldog

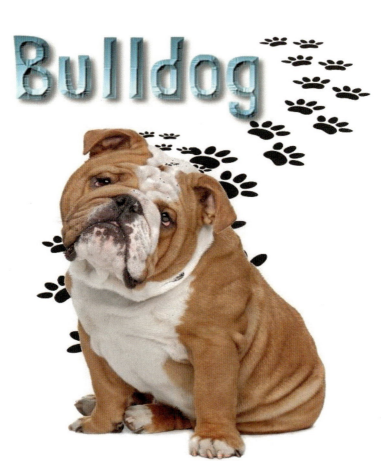

When **you** **first** **see** **a** **Bulldog**, you may think it's mean but they are actually very nice and big couch potatoes. They have lots of wrinkles all over them. Some Bulldogs have an under bite. Bulldogs are originally from England. They live for 3-10 years. Mature Male Bulldogs weigh from 45-55 pounds. Mature Females weigh 45 pounds.

Cairn Terrier

The Cairn Terrier is spirited, bold and inquisitive. They are known for their energetic and curious nature. They are excellent with children and make loving family members. They are particularly valued for their courage, agility, speed and ability to scurry after vermin. Cairn Terriers have a well-proportioned body, not heavily built, with short legs. They can range from the colours cream through red or gray to almost black.

Cavalier King Charles Spaniel

The Cavalier is affectionate, playful and intelligent. The Cavalier was named after King Charles II. These dogs love to explore and play, and their intelligence and eagerness to please means that they respond well to training. The Cavalier is small and well balanced. Their coat is long and very silky. Their colour can be ruby, black and tan, blenheim (a rich chestnut and white mix) and tricolour (black, white and tan).

Chihuahua

The Chihuahua is the smallest dog in the world. The Chihuahua can have two head shapes: apple head or deer head. It is extremely lively, enterprising and proud. The breed is named after the Mexican state of Chihuahua. The Chihuahua is considered the oldest dog on the North American continent. The Chihuahua comes in lots of colours including red, white, chocolate and black, but fawn is the most common colour.

Chow Chow

The Chow Chow is intelligent, independent and protective. Amazingly, the breed has blue-black tongues, not pink. The Chow Chow looks like a big fluffy bear. The Chow Chow is strong, muscular and heavy boned. The head is large, with a broad, flat skull and short, deep muzzle. The Chow Chow comes in five colours: red, black, blue, cinnamon and cream.

Dachshund

The Dachshund is an intelligent, energetic and brave breed. The Dachshund are badger hunters. That's where they got their name. Dachs means badger and hund means dog. Dachshunds are also known as wiener dogs and are short and long. They are smart, courageous and active. The Dachshund presents in all colours.

Jack Russell Terrier

Jack **Russell Terriers are small** dogs that are black, brown and white. They are energetic and very high jumpers. It depends on how much Jack Russell Terriers weigh and how much energy it has to jump high. Jack Russell Terriers can be about 8-12 inches tall. They weigh about 14-18 pounds.

Keeshond

The Keeshond (pronounced Kays-hawnd) is lively, intelligent, friendly and affectionate. The Keeshond enjoys the playful attention of children. It has a fox-like expression and a squarish body. The Keeshond has a dramatically marked colour: a mix of gray, black and cream.

Lowchen

The name Lowchen is German for "little lion". The Lowchen is an easily managed family pet. It is active, intelligent and obedient. They were named "rarest breed" during the nineteenth century. The Lowchen is a stylish, proud looking dog. The Lowchen can appear in any colour or combination of colours.

Miniature Pinscher

The Mini Pincher (a.k.a. Min Pin) is not related to the Doberman Pinscher. The Min Pin is well known as a brave little watch dog. Researchers estimate the Min Pin is a mix of Dachshund, Italian Greyhound and the shorthaired German Pinscher. Solid red or red stag (red with an intermingling of black hair), blue, black and chocolate all appear, with rust coloured markings on the cheeks, lips, lower jaw, chest, throat, above the eyes, lower forelegs, inside of hind legs, feet, lower portion of hocks and vent region. Toes may have black or brown penciling.

Papillon means "butterfly" in French. It's named that for its butterfly wing-like ears. Male Papillons can weigh 8-10 pounds and are 8-11 inches high. The female is 7-9 pounds and 8-11 inches high. The life span of the Papillon is 17 years. The standard colours are white and black, white and lemon, white and red, white and sable, hound tri-colour, with various markings of black, red, sable, or tan.

Pekingese

The Pekingese is also known as the "Sleeve Dog" because some people would carry them in their sleeve. The Pekingese is loyal and affectionate, which makes them worthy watchdogs. The coat can be any colour except liver or albino.

A Corgi is a small dog originated in Pembrokeshire, Wales. They are famed by being the preferred breed by Queen Elizabeth 2. They can be black-headed, tri-colour, or fawn with white markings. Males can be 25-30 pounds and females can be 23-28 pounds. Pembrokes can be 10-12 inches from their feet to the top of their shoulders.

Pomeranian

Pomeranians are small and very furry dogs. They are originally from Germany. They can live to be 12-16 years old. Adults are about 3-7 pounds and are about 11 inches tall. Pomeranians can be red sable, cream and black.

Pug

Pug might be short for pugnus which means "fist" in Latin. A Pug's round face is full of wrinkles so it looks like a clenched fist. It is about 10 inches tall, weighs 14-18 pounds and is originated from Tibet. The Pug can be tan and black, grey and black, or all black.

Russian Toys look like Chihuahuas but are not Chihuahuas. Russian Toys can be 3-6 pounds and are 8-10 inches tall. They are originally from Russia. They can be black, tan, blue, brown, sable or shades of red. The average life span of a Russian Toy is 10-12 years.

Scottish Deerhound

The Scottish Deerhound is gentle and extremely friendly. The breed is famed for being docile and eager to please, with a bearing of gentle dignity. Height of males from 30 to 32 inches or more, weight 85 to 110 pounds; height of females from 28 inches upwards, weight from 75 to 95 pounds. It is one of the tallest sighthounds, with a harsh 3-4 inch long coat and mane, somewhat softer beard and moustache, and softer hair on breast and belly.

Shetland Sheepdogs

Shetland Sheepdogs (a.k.a. Shelties) are known as herding dogs. They can be 16-20 pounds and 13-16 inches. They originate from Scotland. Their average life span is 12-13 years. The litter size is 4-6 puppies. They can be bi-black, bi-blue, sable, mahogany sable, tri-coloured, shaded sable, blue merle, bi-blue merle, sable merle, colour headed white, and double merle.

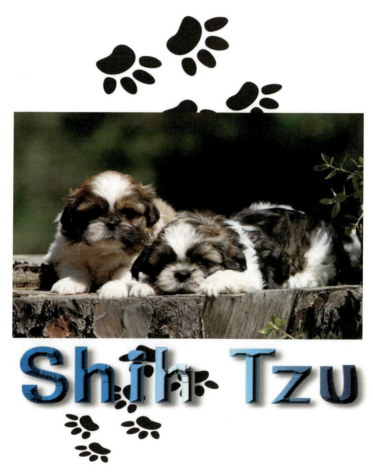

Shih Tzu

I used to have two Shih Tzus named Pixie and Cooper. Shih Tzu are small furry dogs that can be brown, white, black, grey, gold and brindle red. Their litter can have 1-8 puppies. A Shih Tzu can be 10-16 years old. They weigh about 16 pounds and can be 7-11 inches. Shih Tzus originate from China.

Yorkshire **Terriers** (aka Yorkies) are small, furry black and brown dogs. They have a high pitched bark. They originate from England. Yorkies can live to be 10-15 years. two popular Yorkie names are Lady and Princess.

Thank you for purchasing this ebook, the author would be most grateful if you would be kind enough to leave a review.

Facebook page
https://www.facebook.com/pages/Brae-Lynne/703659583025293

About the Author

Brae Lynne is nine years old and lives with her parents, her younger brother, Brody, their Bernese Mountain Dog, Kaiser, who thinks he's a lap dog, a long-haired orange tabby fluff-ball, Carrot, who is the neighbourhood socialite, and a fat black and white feline, Georgie. Her favourite animals are dogs, owls, sea otters, baby harp seals, and turtles. Her favourite colour is green. She loves to play piano. This is her first book, but she intends on writing more.

A portion of the sales will be donated to an animal shelter in her home town to support the care of needy animals.

COLORING BOOK

Please support animal shelters in your community.

Made in the USA
Charleston, SC
06 December 2014